On the Prowl

Contents

On the Prowl with Cheetahs

Written by Terry Miller Shannon

I study cheetahs.
One day, I watched
a cheetah hunt for food.
I will never forget it!

4:00 P.M.

The cheetah's spots
help her hide.
But I see her.

We stop the jeep.
Cheetahs are shy.
We don't want
to scare her.

Cheetah comes from the Hindi word *chita*.
It means "spotted one".

3

4:15 P.M.

The cheetah sees her prey.
It is an animal.
The cheetah watches.

4

4:20 P.M.

The cheetah still watches.
She steps forward.
She is very quiet.
She creeps closer and closer
to the animal.

Cheetahs are the fastest cats. They can run over 95 kilometres per hour.

4:28 P.M.

Now the cheetah runs.
She races so fast.
She looks as if she is flying!

6

The cheetah trips her prey.
The animal falls down.
The cheetah bites its neck.
She chokes it.
The animal dies.

4:45 P.M.

The cheetah eats her meal.
She is very tired.
But she must watch for
lions and other animals.
They will want to steal her food.

Fewer than 12,500 cheetahs are left. These cats are now an endangered species.

4:50 P.M.

The cheetah hisses at a lion. Now it is the lion's turn to be on the prowl!

Jumping Hunters

Written by Lisa Trumbauer

Imagine a creature with eight legs.
It has two big fangs.
It has eight creepy eyes.
Look out!
It jumps to attack.

Is it an alien from outer space?
No! It lives right here on Earth.
It is the jumping spider.

The jumping spider has good eyesight.
Its front two eyes are almost like binoculars.

Jumping spiders come in many sizes.
Some are tiny. Some are big.
At least, they seem big—for a spider.

Many spiders spin webs.
Not this spider.
It doesn't need a web to catch food.
It jumps on its prey!

Most jumping spiders are small,
about the size of a pencil rubber.

Jumping spiders can jump many times
further than the length of their body.

The jumping spider
makes a silky string.
It sticks the string
to a wall or a plant.
It's like having a safety rope.
The spider jumps.
Then it climbs back up the string.
It moves like Spider-Man!

But the jumping spider
is not a superhero.
It doesn't jump to the rescue.
It jumps to eat.
And it rarely misses!

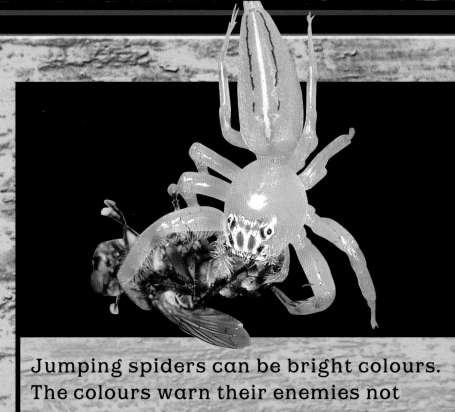

Jumping spiders can be bright colours.
The colours warn their enemies not
to eat them, because they taste bad.

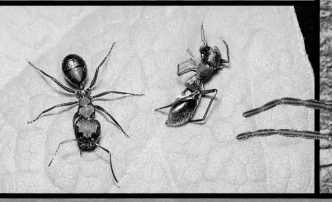

This jumping spider looks like an ant,
but it has eight legs, not six!

The jumping spider is a meat eater.
Insects are on its menu.
It creeps up on the insect slowly.
Then—pounce! Dinner!

Falcons
Runway Rescuers

Written by Lisa Trumbauer

Birds are not welcome at airports.
They can get sucked into a plane's engines.
They can crash into the windscreen.
Birds mean danger to planes.
And planes mean danger to birds.

Birds and aeroplanes are a dangerous mix.
If they collide, the planes may be damaged;
the birds may die.

One kind of bird is welcome at an airport.
Falcons help keep other birds
away from the runways.

Tom Cullen works with falcons at a big airport.
He is a falconer.
We asked him how his birds can help keep runways safe.

Tom Cullen

Q. How do falcons clear birds from runways?

A. Many birds are afraid of falcons.
They can tell when a falcon is hunting.
They will try to get out of the falcon's way.

Q. Do you train the falcons to do this?

A. A falcon knows how to hunt.
I train it to act as if it is hunting when I ask it to.

Trained falcons wear hoods over their eyes when they are not flying. The hoods help keep the birds calm.

Q. Do the falcons kill the birds?

A. No. They just scare birds away.

Q. How well does this work?

A. It works very well. Some birds will stay almost 1.6 kilometres away.

A falcon dives and swoops at other birds to clear them from airport runways.

Dog on Duty

Falcons aren't the only ones with "eagle eyes"! At some airports, dogs are used to frighten off birds. This is Jet. He is on runway duty.

The wide, open area of an airport is a natural attraction for birds.

Q. Where do you get the falcons you train?

A. We raise them from eggs.
They hatch while in the care of people.

Falcon eggs usually take about 30 days to hatch. Chicks that are fed by hand get used to being handled by people.

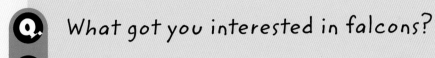

Q. What got you interested in falcons?

A. When I was young, I saw a movie. The kid in the movie had a falcon. I was hooked!

Falconers wear leather gloves to protect themselves from the bird's sharp claws.

THE TRUTH ABOUT
SHARKS

WRITTEN BY JACK KIMBLE

Sharks are hunters.
They can bite.
They can kill.
But are all sharks scary?
Get the facts.
Then you can decide.

Hammerhead shark

Blue shark

Whitetip shark

Fact: Sharks do not hunt people.

Sometimes, sharks bite people.
Sometimes, sharks kill people.
But usually they bite only
by mistake.
Some scientists say that sharks
don't like how we taste!

Reef shark

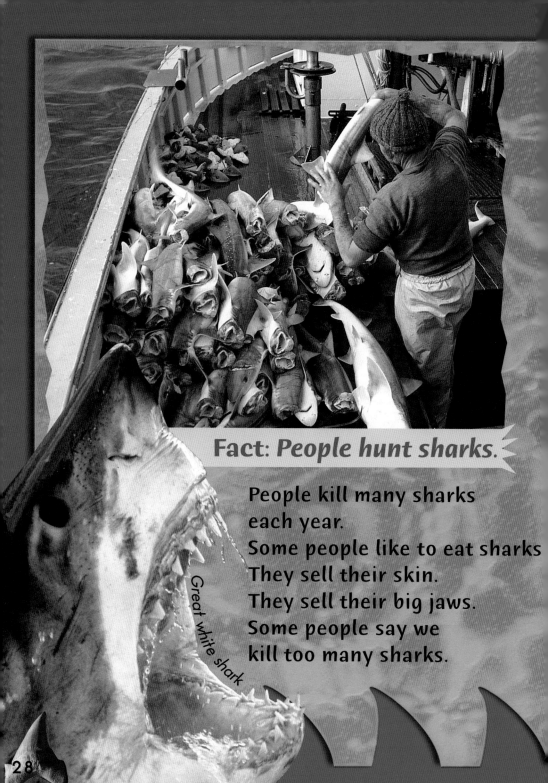

Fact: *People hunt sharks*.

People kill many sharks
each year.
Some people like to eat sharks
They sell their skin.
They sell their big jaws.
Some people say we
kill too many sharks.

Great white shark

Who's the Hunter?

Number of sharks killed
by people each year:
100 million

Number of people killed
by sharks each year:
10 to 15

Some people use dried
shark fins to make soup.

*Sharks hunt seals,
sea lions,
and many
other animals.*

Fact: *Not all sharks bite people.*

There are more than 350 kinds of sharks.
Most kinds of sharks don't bite people.

Whale sharks are
as long as a school bus.
They do not bite people.

Whale shark

Pygmy sharks are
as small as your hand.
They do not bite people.

Pygmy shark

Great white sharks are
the scariest sharks.
They sometimes bite people.

Great white shark

What do you think
of sharks now?

Index